Publisher: Independent Publishing Network
Publication Date: 2021
ISBN: 978-1-80068-091-3
Author: Mollie Plummer (1888 – 1985)
Edited by Elaine Bevis (granddaughter)
Email address: elainebevis@aol.com
Address: 6 Coniston Close, Horsham RH12 4GU
Please direct all enquiries to Elaine Bevis

ISBN 978-1-80068-091-3

Printed in the UK by Short Run Press Ltd

LIFE AND LOVE BELOW STAIRS

AT STANSTED HOUSE

1908 – 1910

Recollections of Mollie Plummer - Head Kitchenmaid

INTRODUCTION

My grandmother, Mary Isobel Plummer (known as Mollie), worked at Stansted House on the borders of West Sussex and Hampshire for the Wilder family from 1908 until the house was closed up in 1910. Many years later she wrote about her time working in service, including her time at Stansted House, and I have used her words together with contemporary postcards and modern views of the house and grounds to give a flavour of life below stairs at that time.

Mollie applied to be head kitchenmaid at Stansted at the age of 20 despite the requirement being 25 years or over. Her three references secured her the post but she had to be very careful from then on not to disclose her true age. Her previous post had been in the Midlands and she was pleased that she would now be closer to her parents in Newick, East Sussex. She was confident that she could cope with the duties required, having now a wide experience in cookery, and she hoped the new post would add to her confidence.

Elaine Bevis

Mollie picks up the story in her own words:

I travelled from Newick by train and was met at the station with a carriage for the journey to Stansted. We soon turned into the big gates and I was told the drive was about two and a half miles to the house. It was a winding and pretty drive teeming with rabbits, turning and bobbing away from the side of the drive, showing their little white tails, and very peaceful, with just the cooing of the wood pigeons and the occasional unseen animal scuttling through the undergrowth. The route was mainly woodland until we reached another lodge. The road then opened up a little and through the trees every now and then you got a glimpse of a magnificent mansion. I had enjoyed my leisurely ride and my companion had given me a description of the place. The house stood in a park of three hundred acres, and the estate was between four and five thousand acres. From the house there was a splendid view of two great beech avenues extending for two miles.

On arriving at the house, I found just the same atmosphere of restfulness as I experienced on my drive from the station. I was introduced to the servants and shown my quarters where I would be working. The housekeeper had left orders that when I arrived, I could be taken to some of the cottages to deliver soup and other good things. There would be very little to do until the end of the week except catering for the staff which I found was my responsibility.

The women servants' sleeping quarters were in the north wing, and we all had beautiful rooms. I shared a very large room with one other. Two lovely Turkish carpets covered the floor and we each had a wardrobe, a chest of drawers and a washstand. There were three good windows. It was quite the most sumptuous accommodation I had ever had.

I had indeed fallen on my feet this time. I was getting another two pounds a year which made my salary twenty pounds a year. The wages at that time were low and you really could not put any aside for safe keeping. There was always something to buy when you got paid in the way of clothes or shoes. In those days we took a great pride in having a drawer full of nicely made underclothes. Then my greatest joy was to buy my little brother and sister a present when I went home. The expectancy was so great that it would have been a tragedy had I gone home empty handed. I also liked to buy my mother something to help with the housekeeping. So, by the time I was to return, my purse was empty, and I would have to borrow from my father to get back. As soon as my wages came, I would return this. But, that was how tight things were. I do not remember it troubling us a great deal – we did not know any different. We were well kept which was the main thing. I often wished I lived a little nearer my home so that I could help my parents with some of the good food that had to be disposed of.

Kitchen Life

The kitchen itself was part of the old house. It was very spacious and lofty with three large long windows looking out on to the Dutch garden – not that we could see out very easily as there was a long charcoal burner under the windows. It was a very nice light kitchen. I had found in the past that it was more usual for the kitchen to have huge skylights in the roof, not unlike a greenhouse, rather than proper windows. The kitchen also had a huge fireplace where one could roast with spits. These were hanging in one part of the kitchen. I was relieved to hear that the spits were no longer used and that all the cooking was done on the big kitchen range. There was a lovely steel hot table with hot pipes running through it. You put the hot dishes on this as you were dishing up. This was cleaned and polished so you could almost see your face in it. Beside this was a hot cupboard where all the lunch china was kept, and at the far end a long dresser almost the width of the kitchen, full of copper saucepans and moulds. From one direction from the kitchen ran the china room and the cooked meat larder, and from another direction, the scullery, and several other larders for meat, game, etc., and through yet another door in another part of this hive of business was the dessert room where the gardeners brought the fruit fresh from the garden daily.

The gardeners grew bananas, oranges, peaches, grapes, and many rare fruits. They would sometimes stop and arrange the dessert dishes for us. Through the dessert room and down a few stairs was the still room where the bread, cakes and preserves were made. I found I was to spend a lot of my time in this room.

I had charge of all the china, of which there was a vast amount. There was a dinner service for every night of the week for a full course dinner for twenty people. There was a Harlequin set with not one plate alike. Even in those days it cost two guineas to replace any plate broken in any of these sets. As they came out of the dining room they were placed in leather buckets and carried to the still room to be washed up. This was my second-in-command's duty. It takes years of training to learn how to handle valuable china. I do not think people realise that all the beautiful china we see in noblemen's houses is still there after perhaps hundreds of years solely to the training of servants of the past. There were some things the old head housemaids would allow no one to move but themselves. The girl whose job it was to look after the washing up of the china was inexperienced and had no inclination to learn. The resultant breakages occurred. Strangely enough the butler replaced all such breakages, but he felt obliged to point out to me that it must stop. So, I took the job on myself. It went very much against the grain on my part to go to the still room after dinner to see a pile of broken plates. No plate was ever sent to the dining room with the smallest chip or crack, and with care it was quite easy to keep them perfect. There were excellent leaded sinks for washing and rinsing, and I am happy to remember that I neither broke nor damaged one piece.

The Dresden china which was used for afternoon tea was in the charge of the menservants. A pile of little muffin shaped plates would be brought to the kitchen for the cakes, biscuits (all homemade, of course), white and brown bread and butter, rolled into tiny Swiss rolls. I remember one day a footman brought a pile of these charming little dishes in and put them rather carelessly on the table. They slid the length of the table and fell off the other end. I felt it was a great tragedy, but he could see only the funny side of it. He was one of those people who never let anything worry them. I would rather have died than confess to such carelessness to the butler. This was not because he was a tyrant; he was really a very nice man. He had been with the family all his life, first of all with the parents of the present generation. He kept everyone strictly in their place. Although some felt afraid to approach him, I never felt so. Many a kind word he gave me, and he was always ready to help me with any difficulties I came across.

We had a very good housekeeper, too, who did her full share of work. She was one of those old-fashioned cooks who had worked her way to the top the hard way. Everything she did had a good foundation. We made our own glaze for gravies, and black jack for colouring, baking powder and so on. She was an extremely competent housekeeper and I gained a good deal from her store of knowledge. When she had got me used to the run of the place, she went to Holland for six weeks with a previous employer. I was left in charge with advice and help from the butler. I managed quite well, but she returned in time for Goodwood, which was a very busy time for us all.

Goodwood Races

At the races we had the largest tent on the course, and a most elaborate lunch would be sent down each day of the races. Four menservants would go, and for that week one extra man for the dining room was engaged. There would be about twenty staying in the house, and there were usually two or three in the dining room for lunch.

The rule was that all the gentlemen came to the dining room for breakfast, but the ladies had breakfast on a tray in their rooms, which was, of course, all very dainty. The dining room breakfast was a feast. There would be four hot dishes, as well as boiled eggs, and all the usual cold meats laid out on the sideboard. There would also be a display of home-grown fruit.

At such times we have been up until three o' clock in the morning preparing for the following day - decorating small moulds with minute pieces of vegetables. For things that were set in aspic jelly, the result was well worth the time and trouble taken.

My French cooking experience was paying dividends during

this very smart week when everything had to be of the very best. Four very large boxes, rather like butlers' trays but deeper, went to the course each day, and we were known to have the best table on the course. When we had seen the lunch go off, we got down to preparing the evening dinner which was very grand and elaborate. It often involved the most complicated sweet courses. We knew exactly what we had to do, as the housekeeper would have to prepare the menus for the week beforehand and Madam would pass them; it was very rare that she altered anything.

The dressmakers were busy weeks before in the workroom. So many dresses had to be made for wearing on the course and at dinner. The same dress was never worn twice. In fact our Lady had never been known to wear any dress more than three times. She was very pretty and looked wonderful in anything. They were a very happy couple and this happiness was felt throughout the house. The squire was young in his ways and full of fun. He possessed two lovely cars[i], one of which was large enough to set lunch in the back. This was often done when they went for a long drive together. I remember Madam once said that in the twelve years they had been married, they had never been apart one night. I think that was true. I know that if the squire missed his train from London, he would come down by special - this would have cost him fifty pounds.

My firm intention was to spend my life in service. I was, in fact, becoming one of those stern old housekeepers, desirous of keeping those under me in their place and endeavouring to get them as interested in their work as I had been. But even then it was not easy and rather hard work for a head servant. No doubt I had also been a headache to those over me in the past. After a while the housekeeper announced she was getting married. This came as a thunderbolt to most of us as she was accepted as being at the old maid stage. She married a very nice man of her own age and settled down very quietly. I got the time off and my eldest brother and I went to the wedding.

Time passed and Goodwood came around again. As it was such an important affair, I suggested we should have an extra professional, so a cook housekeeper was engaged. Things didn't work out and I was asked to take on the housekeeper's responsibilities for the Goodwood season. Fortunately we had a very good intelligent woman who always came to help out. She had been trained in the kitchen, so instead of her wasting time washing up in the scullery, I brought her in as first kitchen maid. She was excellent; you could be working at the table and she would anticipate the article you would need next. With the help and encouragement of the butler, everything went through without a hitch until the end of the week. I gained in confidence and with my varied experience I could have taken any post from there, but the funny thing was that no one had any desire to move on. There were under-maids who had no wish to move, although it would have been to their advantage to do so. Life was very good for one and all.

The House Itself

The house was magnificent although it was not the original. I understood there had been two houses on this site before, both having been burnt down[ii]. The young squire and his wife set about the rebuilding and spent three years abroad collecting treasures to furnish it. They made a wonderful job in rebuilding the house. The main hall, for instance, took three years for the modelling of the cupids and fancy work to be completed. There were life-sized statues of a pair of fairly large dogs, and of a woman in white marble which caught your eye as soon as you entered. At night it was lit by electric bulbs in the colour of the day. If red was the colour, silk rose shades would be clipped over the bulbs. The electricity was generated on the estate, and it was said there were five thousand lights[iii].

The large dining room was entirely lit by electricity. It had an extraordinary clock on the far wall which lit up from the inside and told the time, rising and setting of the sun, and the moon's activities. It was all done by electricity. All these beautiful rooms had lovely long windows - they had just two huge panes of glass in them. The big dining room was mainly green and gold, with electric bulbs round the cornices in the ornaments of the walls. The red dining room was smaller and intended for use when the family were alone. That seldom happened when they were in residence so it was hardly used for if the lady happened to be alone for lunch, she would have something simple on a tray served in her boudoir to save the men a little trouble. The red dining room was hung with the most exquisite curtains, and the pull-down blinds were of beige ruched silk. The whole house was fitted with these blinds, even the servants' hall. This was a very large comfortable room with a parquet floor, so that only the rugs had to be rolled away for dancing.

There were two drawing rooms, a large library which was a real man's room with its large cabinet of expensive cigars and thousands of cigarettes which all and sundry seemed to enjoy.

No doubt the squire would tell them to help themselves as he was a most generous man.

I have mentioned the inner hall before, this had a grand piano and an organ, which at that time would cost £600. From there one ascended a wide staircase to the next floor where the bedrooms all had their own dressing and bathrooms, leading from one another. The walls were padded with the colour of the suite in satin, and the ceilings were very grand. I remember on entering the bathroom of Madam's suite, I felt I was in a garden. There was no sign of a bath or the various things you might look for, but each and every thing was disguised as a garden chair or seat with the deepest green carpet I had ever seen, just like a green lawn. The rest of the suite was a soft pink with a large oak canopied bed.

From these many rooms one carried on up more stairs to the bachelors' floor which was arranged for single gentlemen. The corridors were richly carpeted and the entrances to the rooms were rounded archways hung with coloured beads to the floor which jingled rather prettily as you parted them to enter the room. Huge palms stood at each side of the archway. This floor was rather hidden from the outside by a balustrade surrounding the top of the house. From the inside of the house you could walk for quite a distance as on a terrace. You had wonderful views and from the south side looked out to sea. Sometimes the ships out at sea would turn their searchlights in our direction and on a dark night it was a wonderful sight to behold when they rested on the house. It stood out so clearly.

The top and bottom floors of the house were in a way hidden, although the latter being built below the level of the house, was so arranged that all windows looked up a grassy slope and then on to the balustrade which was built as a seat. On that floor was the housekeeper's room, servants' hall, pantry with a large safe, the butler's bedroom and many cubicles for menservants. Underneath this floor were the cellars for wine, etc., and it was just like an ice house.

There was a wide cobbled stone courtyard running the whole length of the North Wing, with the staff quarters on one side and the stables on the other. In the centre on white pillars was a fine stable clock. You would often see the squire in this courtyard cleaning his own car. Although he must have been thirty, he was just like a jolly school boy. I was coming along this courtyard one day when his head came out from under a sports car with a 'hello', and such a nice smile. There were plenty of people to do such work, but I expect it was a change for him to get dirty.

The front entrance to the house was on the west side, and at the top of a wide sweep of stone steps, there was quite a good-sized space for chairs, etc. and a group of twelve columns. On top of this was a balustrade which the ballroom opened onto. (The ballroom had a dais for the band and the walls were mirrored.) The design on the east side was exactly the same. On the south side there was no door but two flights of steps onto a terrace where surmounting the balustrade were fifteen garden plant ornamental vases, resembling huge rose bowls on stands which were always in bloom except in winter.

The family crest was artistically worked over the west and east portals, and a tall glass structure with a dome on the top went up from the centre of the house and from which the flag was flown when the family were in residence. This would be hauled down when they were away. Except when there was a week's shooting, the races or hunting, they were rarely in residence from Tuesday to Friday. We never minded the weekend being full of company as we always had the mid-week break to look forward to. It was really a place in a thousand. We could play bowls, cricket and croquet, or go to the nearest town, Portsmouth.

The Church

We had our own private church about a stone's throw from the house. The pews for the squire and his guests were in front, but curtained off from the rest of the congregation. There was none of the compulsion to attend I had experienced in my previous situations. About a mile away, still on the estate, was another church, and the vicar alternated between the two. No doubt the church had played an important part in the lives of the squire's ancestors. There were stories about how strict the squire's mother had been. By all accounts it had not been the happy house we all had the good fortune to enjoy. She had a bell by her bedside which she rang at six o' clock each morning into the staff quarters in the north wing. She would then proceed to take a walk from her part of the house to ensure that everyone was rising. Woe betide you if you were still in bed! In our time, however, she lived quietly in the Dower House.

Folly

There was another ruin on the estate, Racton Tower, a banqueting hall built a couple of centuries previously. How they got to it from the house is a mystery to me. It would be wonderful to be able to slip back into the past and witness some of the jollifications that went on. It was a very interesting place and your imagination could run riot. It looked out to sea and I could imagine it being used as a look-out. The top of the tower had gone, and five stories of the centre tower and the two smaller columns on either side were very broken. The inside was hollow with initials cut in the stone all over the place. We often went to this ruin that had seen so many gay times and which now was so calm and peaceful.

The grounds

We found some lovely walks, but the estate extended so far that I do not believe we ever went outside it. You could roam for hours through the lovely green shady rides which were maintained by the keepers for the shooting parties and their own convenience. The grass was like velvet, probably kept short by the rabbits.

I read in a periodical about fifty years ago that there were fifty acres of garden and ten acres of glass houses. I feel the latter was rather exaggerated, but there was a good deal of glass - there was a tropical house, white and black grape houses, banana house, orangery, and a wide expanse of peaches under glass planted in the style of an orchard. There must also have been many plant houses.

I could never understand why the Bothy where the young gardeners lived was so antiquated; it sorely needed bringing up to date to be more in line with its surroundings.

Except for the Dutch garden which was on the east side of the house, there were no laid out gardens round the house. The approach from two sides was just perfect velvet lawns. One then passed through a gate into a land of colour and delightful garden scents.

Cricket[iv]

There had been a cricket match the day I arrived and the squire and his lady and the visitors had left until the end of the week. I saw some of the staff sitting at ornamental garden tables in front of the house where the cricket pitch - a large expanse of beautifully mown lawn - stretched into the distance. The young squire was a very keen cricketer and had his own cricket XI. He also kept his own professional bowler in residence for the season. The fixtures were all arranged at the beginning of the season so that we knew exactly how to cater. There would be a large marquee erected on the lawn in which lunch would be served. There would be one hot dish only and the rest cold. There would be chickens, ducks and all kinds of cold meats, vegetables and salads, steak and kidney pies. The visiting teams were often most interesting as the fixture would coincide with a ship coming into port. After the match was over it was a job to keep the sailors out of the house, especially the kitchen. It was a welcome change to all those young at heart tucked away in the country, beautiful though it was. When all had gone and the tent was cleared, it was often a problem to know what to do with what was left. There might be a dozen chickens with only the breasts carved. All we could make use of would be three or four legs to devil for breakfast or for a chaudfroid for lunch. Anything left over for the servants' hall was out of the question. However, I soon found an appreciative source.

The Gardeners and a blossoming friendship

Several of the single gardeners who lived in a bothy in the gardens did their own housekeeping and I was glad to be able to help them. Their wages were very low. Hungry, hard-working fellows could not have had much left at the end of the week and I am sure they were very glad of an extra tuck in. We also had a great deal of bacon which we could not use, such as the streaky. Rather than let it go in the pig tub, I would pass that on.

There was a flower room in the house where the four indoor gardeners worked in the afternoons. There was a great deal of flower decorating in the house to be done. There were two dining rooms and when dinner was served in the big dining room, the gardeners traced the table. Also, a very choice plant was let into a cavity on each corner of the table. After dinner the head gardener would come to remove his precious plants.

At this time I met my future husband, but I did not know so as first. I first saw him the day I arrived at this place. He was coming from the house with a gentleman's cricket bag which had been left behind after the cricket match. Although he was working on the estate, I did not see him again for six months. Then, one evening as we were being driven in the staff van to a concert, I sat next to him, thinking no more of each other than fellow servants. It then happened that the head housemaid wanted me to meet her at the station at 9 o'clock as she did not like coming home in the dark. I started out in good time to meet her, but when I got out of the open part of the drive and under the trees, it was so dark that I was afraid to go another step. I could not even see the sky, so I got back into the open part and went back the way I had come and on to the gardens. I went to the bothy and asked if there was anyone who could come with me.

A very nice young man came forward. He looked about eighteen but was in fact twenty-three. He was used to walking through this particular part of the wooded drive. From that time, I think we must have arranged to meet again as we went for many enjoyable walks, finding pleasure in each other's company. I could not tell him then that I was hardly twenty-one as I had come to the place as over twenty-two. I had to be so careful not to give myself away. I found it very difficult at times. Birthday books were very much in vogue at that time and members of the staff would bring their books for the entry of your birthday and the date of birth. If I slipped up, I would be accused of making out I was younger than I was, but following the Registry Office[1] suggestion that I added to my age, I had to retain it for the rest of my time in private service. I never regretted taking this advice as it would have been my loss not to have known this wonderful house and its people.

Now that I had a companion for my free Sundays, we would go further afield than I had been able to go before. One day we came across a large building quite near the house. It was built like a pantheon and was very imposing. On enquiring we found that former squires had used it for theatricals. In our time it was used for storing precious articles collected by the squire and his wife on their tour of thc East. I believe I have read in later years that under its present owner it has been renovated and used as a theatre.

My now constant companion and I went to Portsmouth quite often, occasionally to the Theatre Royal where on one occasion we saw The Merry Widow. There were also two music halls. One could get a wonderful meal for eight pence. To visit the place years later was a strange experience - so many things had changed. We had known it in the days of long skirts trailing the ground. Your right hand would be occupied in holding a

---

[1] The Registry Office referred to here is the agency through whom Mollie was placed in the job

bunch of your skirt off the ground. Some women wore an elastic band on their wrist which was attached to the skirt. The skirts were long enough to hide our ankles from view. We wore Russian braid around the hem of our skirts and dresses, which at that time were very wide. Always after going out there would be the business of cleaning the bottom of your dress. If you lived in the country and could go for a walk on nice short grass, you could let your skirt go and walk in comfort. I say in comfort, but that would be if your tight-laced corsets would allow. Wasp waists and long skirts were the order of the day, with pin toed shoes. What we suffered for fashion! However, I believe it was even worse in my mother's day, when they wore bustles.

Monty the Mastiff and other animals

In the pantry near the safe a French mastiff slept on a raised square platform. Woe betide anyone who tried to enter! The first footman was six feet tall and the dog was even taller when standing on his hind legs. I well remember one night we were having a dance in the servants' hall and the dog returning from his after-supper run heard the excitement down below and leaped from the front portico through a heavy glass skylight, cutting his front legs very badly. The first footman carried him through by embracing him round the chest. I noticed then his hind legs were only just clear of the floor. A vet was telephoned for and 'Monty' was an invalid for a long time. His fore legs were in splints and he was very sorry for himself. The first footman had charge of him and when I wanted to visit him, I would have to ask permission. He was almost human and like all animals liked to be petted. However, when he was well, one had to restrain affection for him as he was liable to take advantage. I daresay the men played with him, but when he jumped and put his front paws to our shoulders it was as much as you could do to stand firm. He was so solid, as he was so well fed.

William and Walter, 1st and 2nd Footmen at Stansted House around 1910 with Monty the mastiff

We also had in the house a Japanese spaniel, a nice little dog but a ladies' pet. There was nothing he liked better than to escape to the kitchen where he would delve into the coal scuttle hoping to find a titbit. Being marked with a white muzzle around his pug nose, you can imagine what a comic picture he made. Of course, the first place he would make for would be my lady's boudoir and to save him getting into a bother I would have to stop what I was doing and wash his face. He was no drawing room dog at heart.

Outside we had two bulldogs - a lady and gentleman. At a later date Monty had a fight with them. Everyone ran to try and part them, but no one succeeded until the squire arrived with a stout stick and brought it down on Monty, injuring his back, which laid him up again for a time. Both bulldogs joined in the scrap, but the puppies that were expected were lost.

I, myself, had two cats, a tabby and a blue Persian. The Persian was given to the lady as a present, but as she was one of those people who freeze when a cat is in the room, it was passed on to me. When the butler brought the box down to me and said he had a present for me, I could not begin to guess. When I opened it and saw that lovely blue ball of fluff, I was in heaven. However, it was unfortunate that the first footman disliked cats and he would set Monty on to them, hoping to get rid of them. The time came when I had to bar the dog from coming into the kitchen. I took great care of these cats. They each had their own comfortable basket in a sitting room adjoining the kitchen.

I remember, after cooking a joint of twenty pounds for the servants' hall, the hall boy unloaded his tray in the kitchen and I suppose he did not notice Monty the dog following him. I went in soon after and Monty had got the greasy mass on my marble floor. I went to grab it, but he was quicker. As he picked it up it unrolled and he disappeared dragging a half yard chunk of meat. It was goodbye to the servants' hall supper, but when you have plenty, and know how, it is simple to improvise.

I must relate another spot of bother Monty once got into. One evening the Lady's maid offered to take him for his night's walk with the pet dog. On rounding a bend in the drive, the steward's car came around at a terrific pace and hit Monty. The car ploughed through an iron fence. It was a dark night and when all was sorted out, Monty could not be found. Searchers were out the best part of the night, calling for him and expecting to find him dead. They continued the search the next day, but no luck. The squire offered a generous reward and after about four days someone reported they had seen him come out of the woods and go back in again. The search began again and what a relief to know he was still alive. He had no doubt been laying up very ill. He was terribly thin and drowsy, and afraid. Not a bit like himself, but he soon recovered. The squire had paid £150 for him, so he was a precious piece of dog flesh!

Monty had the important task of guarding the enormous

amount of silver in the house. The centre piece on the large dining table was solid silver and I remember the menservants telling me it had cost £500. It was in the form of a lily pool surrounded by reeds and pokers - every piece made separately and could be removed for cleaning by a turn of a screw. It was a very handsome piece. Four men were required to remove it bodily.

Life Below Stairs

I remember getting one rather bad fright. The squire and his lady had gone away for a few days. They were not expected home until the following Tuesday and on the Saturday afternoon the whole staff had gone to Portsmouth, except for myself and the second footman. I was sitting at one of the ornamental tables in front of the house, making lace for the latest pile of underclothes I had made, and the footman was having a bath, when through the trees in the distance I thought I recognised our big yellow and black car. I raced across to the Keepers Cottage, or rather Lodge, which was not far from the house to make sure. I was right! There was not a housemaid in the place and the house was in a shroud of dustsheets. Worst of all, was the fact that the big kitchen range had just been made up and was as black as ink. It was the only means of boiling water and cooking we had. I pulled all the dampers out and rushed to the telephone and got some fish and chicken from the fishmonger. He had closed, but as a favour came out with all we wanted. Meanwhile, the footman and I were whipping off the dustsheets. The funny part was that when the front door bell rang, he had no idea who it might be and hurriedly pulled on his trousers and was still drying himself when he opened the door to the squire. The lady was examining my fancywork!

Never again did we get caught like that, although the squire was very nice about it and said they would have dinner half an hour later than usual. The rest of the staff did not come in until ten o'clock that night, and what a surprise they had! The house was a blaze of lights and they were prepared for something untoward. It did upset the weekend rather as most of the staff had plans for a Sunday off, but there it was - it taught one to always be prepared for the unexpected.

Shooting Parties

We had fairly big shooting parties when huge beef steak and kidney puddings would be cooked and packed in hay boxes to keep them hot until they were ready for lunch. The butler and a footman would usually go to serve. A good round of beef would be roasted the day before to cut up for sandwiches for the beaters. How I would enjoy cooking one of those large joints once again.

My Father's Visit

Towards the end of my stay at Stansted my father expressed a wish to come and see me. I mentioned this to the butler and he invited him for a few days. This made me very happy, and while I was busy he was entertained in the pantry. The butler had one of the men's cubicles prepared for him to sleep in. He had a glorious time, but he confided to me later that when Monty with his strong low bark made himself heard in the night, he felt that any minute he would burst into his room. Father never forgot his experience of a gentleman's life with the very best wines and spirits and cigars. He had always been used to a good table, but he had not seen the size of joints we had to cook, and the general extravagance alarmed him. But how he enjoyed it, and it gave him something to talk about for the rest of his life.

Time to Depart

I could have lived there and been happy for ever, but then one day came the news that the squire and his lady were going abroad for big game shooting for quite a long time. This meant the house would be shut up with the butler in charge, and the rest of the staff would have to leave. This was, of course, a bombshell for all of us, but we had about three months' notice. As a result of this tour a quite different feverish activity was set in motion. French dressmakers moved into the work room. Thirty evening dresses were to be made, apart from many other garments. Splendid brass studded cabin trunks were made for these beautiful creations to be packed into. I particularly remember a white velvet evening dress and one in pink velvet. The lady was very nice looking and dark haired, so she must have looked gorgeous wearing them. Her dress account was huge; it ran into thousands of pounds each year.

They were going to take the big car and a wooden structure had to be made for that. There was so much preparation in every direction. The housemaids were busy spring cleaning and covering everything in linen sheets as they finished.

We still found time for a day off now and then. I recall an unforgettable day at the Franco-British Exhibition in 1908 where I particularly remember the Swan boats in the Court of Honour. It was like being surrounded by fairyland out on the blue water. There was the wonderful architecture of the Indian Palace and the Arts Palace and many other Eastern temples. So much time and effort was put into building them and the time was so short before they were dismantled again.

As a parting present we were all given a choice of two sovereigns or a life size photograph of the lady. She was dressed in a long ermine cloak made of five hundred skins which the squire had personally obtained and had made up for her. It was a grand picture in sepia taken on the terrace. Being a practical person, I chose the money, thinking that as I was getting married, it would be more useful. However, I have never ceased to regret this decision as she had been a grand lady to work for.

The day came when we saw the squire and his lady leave for a trip that would take one to two years. The next day the staff and their luggage were each taken to the station that was most convenient for their journey. Three housemaids and I were the last to leave and it all seemed very strange and quiet. The butler was staying and he came up to the fruit room to say goodbye to me. To my amazement, for I had always known him to be a quiet, rather morose man, he put his arms round me and kissed me, mumbling something about how glad he was that I was going to marry the young man who had been my companion. He said he was the best fellow on the place. Tears were tumbling down his cheeks; he was feeling the breaking up very badly. Some thirty years before he had married a housemaid from this house. They had always lived in a cottage outside the estate, but now they would be moving into the house. The silver was sent to the bank, and Monty was put under the charge of the Head Gamekeeper.

So the last of us were standing on the front steps waiting for the luggage van to collect us, not knowing what the future might hold.

Mollie Plummer in 1911

AFTERWORD

The young gardener that Mollie mentions in her recollections, James Taylor, became her husband in 1913 – they were married for 45 years until his death in 1958. I believe Mollie started writing her memoirs after his death when she was in her seventies – a remarkable achievement.

EB

The Wilders hit the headlines in 1912, as described later in Mollie's memoirs.

Whilst I was working for my next employer I saw a copy of the morning's Times of 8th March 1912. To my sorrow I read that the squire of that lovely place we had so unwillingly left was suing for divorce. According to the paper, Madam had become very friendly with a gentleman on board ship to America, and when they arrived at New York, the squire had gone one way and Madam the other. He continued his tour; she remained in New York. He had left instructions with his solicitor to have her watched, and I suppose the result was the application for divorce. She tried very hard to get in touch with him. She even sent him violets for his birthday, as she had done every year of their marriage, but got no reply. She then wrote to him through his solicitor and said the day he got his divorce she would put a bullet through his heart. When that day arrived, she was stopped in the court's corridor by the police and in her muff, they found a small pistol. She was arrested. During the case the Judge said the squire had been most generous, saying he would pay the insurance on her jewels and give her a substantial allowance, if she would promise to stay out of England. I am quite sure she suffered a great deal as she was very much in love with him.

The result of all this was that the beautiful house with its wonderful treasures and priceless tapestries was sold. It was a four-day sale and no doubt the valuable contents were scattered all over the world.

We heard later that the squire married again, a society lady, and in the 1914 War he was driving a Red Cross car in Spain. The dear old butler obtained another post near Horsham. That was the last we heard. They would have all passed away from this world long ago, but during our stay with them a nicer, happier couple it would have been impossible to meet.

END-NOTES

[i] In 1900 the Wilders met a young man named Claude Grahame-White who was of their own age and who had already become deeply involved in the automobile industry and was planning to move into motor dealership; they persuaded him to go to Paris and buy them some cars. When he returned with the cars, he quickly taught them both to drive and during that time they became firm friends, so much so that George Wilder offered Grahame-White the position of estate manager. He soon made a success of the role, turning a loss into profit in his first year. With the estate in good hands the Wilders departed on an eighteen-month world tour, during which they bought many ornaments for the newly rebuilt Stansted House. When they returned Grahame-White organised a magnificent gala concert and firework display. Grahame-White had always felt that estate management was not his long-term ambition and so reluctantly the Wilders accepted his resignation and presented him with a £1,000 bonus. Grahame-White subsequently became an aviation pioneer taking part in many of the early flying challenges and then acquiring land at Hendon to develop as Hendon Aerodrome.

[ii] The first Mansion was built in 1686 by the 1st Earl of Scarborough and was altered in 1781 by Richard Barwell, a new owner. The 18th century house burnt down in 1900 on the last day of the Goodwood Races.

[iii] The electric lighting Mollie describes was installed by Claude Grahame-White whist he was managing the estate. It was housed in an outbuilding close to the main house and was ahead of its time, coming barely 20 years after the first installation of domestic electricity at Cragside House.

[iv] Cricket was a big passion of George Wilder. He had a cricket pitch in front of the house and ran his own team playing

teams from local estates and villages. Wilder captained his team and usually batted first but this was not pure conceit as he had played for Sussex occasionally. His friend and estate manager Claude Grahame-White often joined the team and Wilder managed to include in his team County and International players such as John Elicius Benedict Bernard Placid Quirk Carrington Dwyer (E B Dwyer). Coincidentally Mollie's fiancé Jimmy Taylor, who was one of the gardeners at Stansted, was descended from the Beldham family, their most illustrious ancestor being Silver Billy Beldham who played for Hambledon, Hampshire, Surrey and England; sadly, there is no record of Jimmy turning out for Stansted House.